VERMONT ROYSTER

THE AMERICAN PRESS
AND THE
REVOLUTIONARY TRADITION

Delivered at
Dinkelspiel Auditorium, Stanford University,
Stanford, California
on
March 6, 1974

American Enterprise Institute for Public Policy Research
Washington, D. C.

© 1974 by American Enterprise Institute
for Public Policy Research, Washington, D. C.

ISBN 0-8447-1308-2

Library of Congress Catalog Card Number L.C. 74-78944

Printed in the United States of America

Among the many revolutionary ideas to emerge from the American Revolution, none proved more revolutionary than the idea of freedom of the press. None has proved more durable, for it has withstood two centuries of assault. None has brewed more controversy, for it remains today even in this country as revolutionary an idea as it was in the eighteenth century and in its American form it exists now only in this country. And of the many changes which time has worked on the political ideas of the Founding Fathers, none would more surprise them—and perhaps disturb them—than what has evolved in the succeeding two centuries from their views of what constitutes freedom of the press. All the evidence suggests that when they embraced this philosophical idea, and embodied it in the First Amendment to our Constitution, they knew not what they wrought.

Certainly when they spoke of freedom of the press they did not envision a press of very nearly unrestrained license, which is for all practical purposes the legal privilege of the twentieth century American press. That idea was foreign to the liberal philosophers, mostly those of the seventeenth and eighteenth centuries, from whom they drew their concepts about the nature of man and society on which they founded the American political system. Nor was there anything in their own experience, even in the midst of rebellion against a distant government, that led them to suppose a civil liberty, whatever its nature, could be severed from civic responsibility and therefore from all restraint. They thought this

1

especially true when one liberty—or, if you prefer, one unalienable right—clashed with another. In few things were they absolutists. So in their view this freedom of the press, as every other freedom, existed only within certain parameters of responsibility, not always precisely definable but existing nonetheless.

Even in our own time the idea of freedom of the press without restraint, which is what that freedom often appears to have become, is disturbing to many people. It is not merely that this freedom is irritating to our governors, although there are many examples of that. It is also disturbing at times to philosophers, to men of the law, to the citizenry generally and not least to some of those within the press itself. Not only is the performance of the press criticized, but the very extent of its freedom is questioned, both from within and from without. So it is that the right to speak and to spread abroad whatever one wishes remains to this day a revolutionary idea; that is to say, one which has not yet lost its controversial nature through unquestioning acceptance.

Yet we have come to accept so much of this idea of freedom of the press that we are scarcely aware of how far we have come from its beginnings. The parameters within which we today debate possible, or desirable, restraints on the freedom to publish, or the terms in which we discuss the need for both a free and responsible press, are quite different from those used by Mr. Jefferson, Mr. Madison or Mr. Franklin. They would have some difficulty, I suspect, comprehending the recent controversy over the Pentagon Papers; they would be puzzled by the near-disappearance of private libel from the canons of the law, or the total disappearance of seditious libel, not to mention the untrammeled performance of the press in the Watergate affair. Certainly they would be aghast at today's license, under the shelter of the First Amendment, for published pornography.

Nonetheless, that we have come so far is in part a logical extension of those very ideas about man and society and the nature of political freedom that permeated the thinking of those who embarked on the American experiment. Just as other of their ideas set in motion political events they did not fully anticipate, so it was here. Their declaration that all men are created free and equal inevitably led not only to the abolition of slavery but to universal suffrage and to an ever-widening concept of civil rights. So with the declaration that freedom of speech and of the press shall not be abridged. That declaration once made, it became ever more difficult to find a point of abridgment.

There is also, however, another reason why in the area of political reporting and publishing the American press has pushed the borders of permissible freedom beyond those in any other country including countries which share our heritage of general political liberty, such as Great Britain itself. That reason lies in geography, that in the time before and during our rebellion the colonies were both remote from the mother country and separated even from each other. Geography made restraints less practical, the opportunities for freedom of expression more available.

Ideas fertilized the American Revolution; it would hardly have come without them. Geography made its success possible; it was the great gulf of ocean that, in the end, made it impossible to put down. These same two things, ideas and geography, also provided the soil for the revolutionary tradition of the American press, a tradition suspicious of all government and fiercely opposed to all restraint. In the two centuries since, it has proved a lasting tradition.

The ideas here involved, as so many others, might be traced back to the Greeks when Plato and Aristotle were debating the nature of man and of government. We are heirs of them both, teacher and pupil, but in politics more Aristotelian than Platonist. It was Plato, after all, who would have had the state lay down rigid rules for poets and philosophers and who would have had their works submitted to magistrates to decide whether they were fit for the people. As we shall see, there are Platonists among us yet. Aristotle, though he defended the slavery of his times and was fearful of pure democracy, did broach the thought that the citizens exercising their collective judgment had the right not only to choose their leaders but to call them to account. The echoes of this are heard in that Declaration of 1776; they reverberate today whenever there is heard a clamor in the press to impeach a President.

But it was the Reformation, with its revolt against the authority of the Church, that more immediately opened the Pandora's box and let escape the idea that each man had a right to make "free inquiry" with his own mind. The inquiry began about God; it was not long before it extended to the state.

Not long, but slowly all the same. In England, which is the principal source of our political heritage, the sixteenth century had ended with absolutism triumphant. By the end of the seventeenth century, having suffered the absolutism of Cromwell, England was a ferment of liberal ideas. The Declaration of Rights of 1689, forced upon William and Mary as the price of their crowns, foreshadows in many particulars not only our own Declaration of Independence but later provisions in our Constitution; it proclaimed among other things that at least in Parliament there must be freedom of debate.

This was the century, too, of John Locke, with his thesis of popular sovereignty under which government was merely the trustee of power delegated by the people and which the people could withdraw. And the century of John Milton, who in his *Areopagitica* argued that men can distinguish between right and wrong ideas if these are allowed to meet in open encounter. Locke sowed the seed of rebellion, Milton the seed of the First Amendment in our Bill of Rights.

Still, at the beginning of the eighteenth century they were seeds only. Milton, like Locke, spoke a minority view. Moreover Milton himself, whose motivation was irritation at Puritan censorship of his own theology, would not extend the full freedom of expression to Roman Catholics or to insidious pamphleteers and journalists. And no matter how majestic his argument, it had small effect even upon the intellectual men of his time and none at all upon the political authorities. In England, as elsewhere, the printing press remained subservient to the needs of the state. When the first small cracks did appear in the system of press control—and here, of course, we are speaking primarily of books and pamphlets, not newspapers as we know them—those cracks were caused less by the pressure of ideas than by the practical difficulties of enforcement.

Until well into the seventeenth century the printing press was controlled in England by a system of patents, that is, licenses. The Crown gave patents to a group of printers organized into the Stationers' Company. This company had the power to admit and expel members from the printing trade and to discipline the members for such transgressions as might be charged against them by the authorities. For some 200 years this system worked well in controlling the printing press, the Stationers' Company being

4

assiduous in protecting its monopoly. It began to break down only as technology made printing presses cheap and therefore readily available. By the beginning of the eighteenth century the proliferation of presses had made it impossible to enforce the licensing system and equally impractical for an official censor to read and approve every piece of printed matter before it was published. Practicality, then, demanded both a different system and a different rationale, legal and philosophical, to justify it.

The English answer to this problem was both ingenious and far-reaching in its effects. Necessity forced the abandonment of prior restraint on publication. In its place was substituted the idea that the printer, while he could not be restrained in advance, could be held accountable afterwards for what he caused to be published. Gradually what could not be prevented came to be hailed as an unalienable right; what could be adjudicated came to be accepted as a proper restraint upon that right. In time this new concept of freedom of the press, its extent and its limitations, was debated and shaped by men as varied as Dr. Samuel Johnson and Sir William Blackstone.

Blackstone, most especially. For this English jurist not only capsuled the new philosophy and the new law on the press in his famous *Commentaries* but he was also the great teacher for the law-minded revolutionists in the colonies. Today few lawyers read his *Commentaries,* even as a classic, but in the latter part of the eighteenth century and through much of the nineteenth his influence on American jurisprudence was immense, far greater here indeed than in his own country. Before the advent of law schools every budding lawyer began his reading with Blackstone as his guide and oracle. His *obiter dicta* on the common law were pervasive among those who launched and nurtured our experiment in political liberty.

In his *Commentaries,* first delivered as lectures in 1758 and formally published in 1765, a decade before Bunker Hill, Blackstone defined the freedom of the press this way:

> The liberty of the press is indeed essential to the nature of a free state; but this consists in laying no *previous* restraint upon publications, and not in freedom from censure for criminal matter when published. Every

freeman has an undoubted right to lay what sentiments he pleases before the public: to forbid this is to destroy the freedom of the press; but if he publishes what is improper, mischievous or illegal, he must take the consequences of his own temerity.[1]

There, in two sentences, is the whole of the law and the philosophy of the press as it appeared to Englishmen of the eighteenth century, including our own revolutionists.

It is, as you can see, an effort to reconcile the irreconcilable. For plainly if there is to be political liberty the citizens cannot be constrained in what they think and what they speak by the power of government, whether it be a government of a king or of ministers. To subject the press to such restrictions, in Blackstone's words, "is to subject all freedom of sentiment to the prejudices of one man, and make him the arbitrary and infallible judge of all controverted points in learning, religion and government." But also plainly, or so it seemed to the men of those times, no man would be safe and no government secure if all manner of libels could be uttered with impunity. Thus to punish dangerous or offensive writings, said Blackstone, "is necessary for the preservation of peace and good order, of government and religion, the only solid foundation of civil liberty."

It was, perhaps, an unsatisfactory thrust at the Gordian knot to say on the one hand that a man is free to publish what he will without let or hindrance but, on the other hand, that he is not free from accountability for what he publishes, leaving undefined what later may be judged punishable as improper, mischievous or illegal. Yet if that answer seems unsatisfactory to logical minds, it is one we have not bettered two centuries later. In that famous Pentagon Papers case, of which more later, the justices of our own Supreme Court were unable to discard the Blackstonian concept.

However that may be, such was the philosophical view and the legal doctrine about the press and its freedom commonly accepted in those memorable years leading up to 1776. Now, if we are to understand the American press tradition, it is necessary to look at

---

[1] William Blackstone, *Commentaries on the Law of England*, Book 4 (London, 1969), chap. 11, pp. 151ff.

6

the special circumstances in these English colonies which gave those ideas an indigenous cast.

In 1734 the royal governor of the colony of New York was one William Cosby, by the evidence of his contemporaries an avaricious, haughty and ill-tempered man who was among the worst of these representatives of the distant crown. The publisher of the New York *Weekly Journal,* a four-page poorly printed sheet, was John Peter Zenger, an itinerant printer. Before the year was out they were to clash, with consequences neither of them foresaw.[2]

The origin of it, briefly, was a dispute between the governor and the council of the colony over the governor's salary. As part of that dispute Cosby discharged the colony's chief justice, Lewis Morris, and appointed in his place one James Delancey, a royalist supporter. Zenger's print shop issued a pamphlet giving the deposed chief justice's side of the case, and there began a long and acrimonious fight between the royal governor and the *Weekly Journal.* Ultimately, having failed to get an indictment of Zenger from a local grand jury, Governor Cosby had Zenger jailed on his own authority. The charge was seditious libel. Zenger, who had not written the offending articles but who had published them, was refused reasonable bail by the new chief justice and languished in jail for nine months. The next year, 1735, he came to trial.

It was a disappointing trial if the hope was that the issue of freedom of the press from seditious libel would be squarely joined. Zenger's counsel was Andrew Hamilton—not to be confused with Alexander Hamilton—and he saw his task, as lawyers are wont to, to free his client rather than to win some great judicial principle.

---

[2] Frank Luther Mott, *American Journalism,* Third Edition (New York: Macmillan Company, 1962), pp. 31ff, has a good account of the Zenger case, which I have followed. For documents in the case, including Hamilton's defense, see Leonard W. Levy, ed. *Freedom of the Press From Zenger to Jefferson: Early American Libertarian Theories* (New York: Bobbs-Merrill Co., 1966).

Thus Hamilton did not attack the concept of seditious libel. Instead he argued that it was designed to protect the king, not provincial governors, and that if the people could not remonstrate truthfully against despotic governors the people would lose their liberty and the king would be ill served. Then in an impassioned appeal directly to the jurors he asked them, in effect, to ignore the court's rulings on the law and acquit Zenger notwithstanding.

This is what the jury did, quite possibly for no other reason than that Cosby was an unpopular governor and this was a way to strike back at him. Anyway, the Zenger case did nothing to alter the common law of seditious libel nor to advance any new principles with regard to freedom of the press. Nonetheless, the Zenger trial is justly renowned in the history of the colonial press. Cosby vanished in obscurity; Zenger took his place in the pantheon of journalistic heroes. In a very dramatic fashion a small newspaper had challenged royal authority, been brought to trial in a royal court and acquitted by a jury of colonial citizens. That was enough.

There were other cases before and after Zenger, with varying results. As early as 1692 one William Bradford, a Philadelphia printer, had been tried for seditious libel, Thomas Maule for the same charge in Boston in 1696, neither of whom was ultimately imprisoned. But Andrew Bradford, William's son, was later imprisoned for publishing a letter critical of the English government, Benjamin Franklin's brother was jailed for being critical of the Massachusetts colonial government, and also in Massachusetts John Checkley was convicted for distributing a book critical of Calvinist doctrines. Until the eve of the Revolution, there was little consistency, either from time to time or from colony to colony, in the boldness of printers or in the reaction of the authorities to criticism. For the most part, however, boldness was not characteristic of these early printers. Their shops were commercial enterprises; they sought out official business and were inclined to do little to disturb it. They also shared the general attitude of the time, which consisted of much grumbling at particular authority but without any disposition to challenge the principle of authority from the Crown.

This is not the place for recounting the history of the colonial press. It should be noted, though, that the present view of colonial America as a society that everywhere cherished freedom of ideas and expression is a romantic one. There was indeed an enormous diversity of political and religious ideas among the various colonies, due to their origins and geography, and this diversity was ultimately to have an enormous effect. But each colony, sometimes different counties within a colony, had its own orthodoxy and guarded it zealously, being quite willing to suppress the dissidence of the non-orthodox, whether political or religious. In John P. Roche's phrase, "Colonial America was an open society dotted with closed enclaves."

If there was a turning point for the press, a point at which it generally turned rebellious toward the Crown and began to acquire its revolutionary character, it was the same as for the colonists generally, namely, the Stamp Act of 1765. That tax struck very hard at printers. Since it amounted to a penny for each four pages and two shillings for each advertisement, it came to a tax of nearly 50 percent of revenue for many papers. It thus united the printers as no other issue could. The Pennsylvania *Gazette* draped its last pre-tax issue with the black column rules of mourning. The New York *Gazette* openly defied the law by continuing to publish with unstamped paper. A few papers suspended, but many others shifted to irregular publication dates to claim status as handbills not as newspapers. Similar taxes were levied in England and were enforceable. In the colonies, far removed from the home country and with presses scattered over a huge geographic area, the taxes were largely unenforceable.

A year later this Stamp Act was repealed, thanks in good measure to the persuasiveness in London of that Kissinger of the day, Benjamin Franklin. But by then the situation had been permanently altered. Until then the dissatisfaction of most of the printers with the remote government of the Crown had been no more than those generally shared by other colonists; now they had a personal grievance and a warning to what extent they personally could be injured by that remote government. Arguments about the power of government against the press ceased to be abstractions. Equally important—and I am inclined to think more so—the printers learned that in fact this distant government could not enforce its laws against them. Thus the Boston *Gazette,* which in 1765 had printed the bitterest attacks against the Stamp Act, did not relent after its repeal in attacks on Crown government. Indeed, it became even bolder as spokesman for the "radicals," or, if you prefer a different term, for the "patriots."

How much the practical situation had altered is shown by the reaction of the Crown authorities to these new attacks. Governor Bernard of Massachusetts called the *Gazette* "an infamous weekly paper which has swarmed with Libels of the most atrocious kind," made several feeble attempts to get a libel indictment against its publishers, but in the end found it more politic to suffer the paper. He would risk no more Zenger cases. The situation in the other colonies, in varying degrees, was much the same.[3]

Meanwhile, all those other forces which led to 1776 continued to do their work; I will leave to others to decide the proportion in which they were economic, political or philosophical. Slowly but relentlessly the colonists moved from being loyal complainants against particular Crown actions to open rebellion against the Crown itself. Whatever the causes, the movement required a major change in public opinion and in that change the printers of the colony played a major role. Through newspapers, through broadsides, through pamphlets, the printing presses of the colonies proved as dangerous as muskets. The newspapers issued by these presses were outlets for the exchange of information among the colonies (one picking up its "news" from the mailed copies of another), for letters to the editor and for anonymous articles signed with such pen names as Cato or Publius. There was little "objectivity" in the news reported. For example the Salem *Gazette* in its issue of April 25, 1775 began its account of the battles of Lexington and Concord this way:

> Last Wednesday, the 19th of April, the Troops of his *Brittanick* Majesty commenced Hostilities upon the People of this Province, attended with Circumstances of Cruelty not less brutal than what our venerable Ancestors received from the vilest Savages of the Wilderness.

This was the tone of the news reported throughout the Revolution, though often the news was sparse and late due to the difficulties of communication. When there was none many of the printers carried rumors, second and third hand reports and on some occasions seem to have made up their information.

---

[3] Mott, *American Journalism,* p. 75.

But we must not suppose that in this period there had been any advancement in the *philosophy* of freedom of the press. The patriot, or rebel, newspapers had indeed thrown off the yoke of Crown governors, and having got the bit in their teeth made the most of it. The loyalist papers, of whom a few survived even after the war's outbreak, did not fare so well. The patriots were no more anxious to extend freedom of the press to them than the Crown governors had been to extend it to the seditious patriot press. Great pressure, including violence, was exerted to silence the Boston *Evening Post,* the New York *Packet,* and the Maryland *Journal,* all loyalist papers. In an outbreak of mob violence the New York *Gazetteer,* a Tory paper, was totally destroyed. In every faction, freedom of the press meant freedom for *us,* not for *them.*

What did result from the Revolution, if not new philosophies about freedom of the press, were habits and an attitude. The attitude, natural under the circumstances, was one of antagonism to government, or at least distant government; after all, that was the root of the Revolution itself. The habits were of fiercely venting that antagonism without check, at least from any distant government. In a very pragmatic way these two things were to have important consequences. For one, they bestirred a renewed interest among publishers, writers and intellectuals generally in philosophical thinking about the nature of a free press, if for no other reason than to find a respectable rationale for what these writers and printers were in fact doing. The other consequence was that in time the revolutionary habits became transformed into a tradition.

Neither the habits of free-speaking nor the critical attitude toward distant government were, to be sure, limited to printers. Both had been acquired by the former colonists generally. In fact when the Constitutional Convention convened in 1787 the delegates had two problems. One was to devise an acceptable form of national government. The other was to persuade the citizens of the new states to accept *any* national government stronger than the loose Confederation. The extent of this second problem shows up clearly in *The Federalist* papers of Madison, Hamilton and Jay. Again and again while defending the structure of the proposed government they had also to answer critics of the very concept of a national government. Eight of the papers are devoted to explaining the inadequacies of the original Confederation; one (Number 23)

11

is devoted wholly to justifying the need for central government and another (Number 84) to explaining away the need for further checks on the power of the national government. Nonetheless, in the end they had to add such checks, known as the Bill of Rights, in order to get their new government accepted.

One of these checks, embodied in the First Amendment, was that "*Congress* shall make no law . . . abridging the freedom of speech, or of the press" (emphasis added). But this was not then the sweeping doctrine it has since come to appear. The key word then was "Congress"—that is the *national* government was to be prohibited from abridging the press. What was done under state government was to be left to the states; they were not prohibited from regulating the press. Indeed, the Pennsylvania Constitution of 1790 and the Delaware Constitution of 1792 expressly imposed liability for abuses of free speech; even in Virginia a 1792 statute provided sanctions against "abusive" uses of free speech. Thomas Jefferson explained, "While we deny that Congress have the right to control the freedom of the press, we have ever asserted the right of the states, and their exclusive right to do so." [4]

Jefferson, having now made his entrance in our story, is worth a moment's pause. He has, and with some reason, become the patron saint of the press, having proclaimed that if he had to choose between government and no newspapers or newspapers and no government he would do without government. But Jefferson also reflected other views of the press, not untypical of his times. His 1783 draft for the Virginia Constitution provided that the press should be subject to no restraints *other than* "legal prosecution for false facts printed and published." Again, in a letter to Madison he remarked, "A declaration that the federal government will never restrain the presses from printing anything they please, will not take away the liability of printers for false facts printed." [5] That view, as you can see, is essentially Blackstonian; the press should be free of prior restraint but could be liable afterwards for injury by falsehoods. On seditious libel he was ambiguous, or at least changeable. In 1803, angered by its "licentiousness and its lying" he thought the press ought to be restrained by the states if not by

---

[4] Letter to Abigail Adams, September 4, 1804.

[5] Letter to James Madison, July 31, 1788.

the federal government; "I have long thought," he said, "that a few prosecutions of the most prominent offenders would have a wholesome effect in restoring the integrity of the presses." [6] Yet as President he pardoned those convicted under the Sedition Act of 1798. Finally, of course, like all Presidents before or since, he had a low opinion of the performance of the press and angrily assailed the calumnies of the press against himself and against the government. Jefferson, like scripture, can be quoted to one's own purposes.

The next great leap forward for freedom of the press, both in philosophy and in practice, came from that 1798 Sedition Act. This law made it a crime to publish any "false, scandalous and malicious writing" bringing into disrepute the government, the Congress or the President, and it immediately plunged the country into bitter controversy. The press was outraged; victims among newspapers included the New York *Argus,* the Boston *Independent Chronicle,* the Richmond *Examiner.* One of the more famous trials was of Thomas Cooper, who in the Reading *Weekly Advertiser* had called President John Adams an incompetent, and who was imprisoned for six months. Of perhaps passing interest is the fact that at his trial Cooper tried to get Adams as a witness but the court refused to subpoena the President.

The Sedition Act forced Americans to rethink their views on the nature of press freedom. In the Virginia Resolutions against the act, James Madison brought forth a new concept. Noting the common law principle that freedom of the press was limited to imposing no prior restraints on publication, Madison said that could not be the American idea of press freedom since a law inflicting penalties afterward would have a similar effect to a law imposing prior restraint. "It would seem a mockery," he wrote, "to say that no law should be passed preventing publication . . . but that laws might be passed punishing them in case they should be made." [7] And for the first time a loud voice—that of George Hay, prosecutor of Aaron Burr and later a federal judge—was raised to proclaim the idea that freedom of the press was absolute in terms of criticizing the government, whether the criticism be true, false, malicious or

---

[6] Letter to Thomas McKean, February 19, 1803.

[7] Levy, *Freedom of the Press From Zenger to Jefferson,* reprints the text of Madison's argument for freedom of the press (document 28, p. 197).

otherwise. "Freedom of the press," he proclaimed, "means total exemption of the press from any kind of legislative control." He would admit only private actions against the press for private injury, as for any other tort.[8]

These sweeping ideas of Madison and Hay were in advance of their own time. Indeed, it is not fully accepted even yet, Justices Black and Douglas to the contrary, that the press should be free of all accountability to government—that is, to society as a whole—for what it publishes, for in that extreme form freedom of the press raises all manner of political and philosophical questions that are still disturbing. Nonetheless, the outcome of the outcry was that the Sedition Act was repealed. The press emerged freer than ever, its habits of independence and its attitude of suspicion toward government strengthened. The stage was set for the development of the modern American press.

As we approach the last quarter of the twentieth century the American press occupies a unique position. By the word press I refer, of course, not just to the newspapers of mass circulation but to the whole of the press in all its multiplicity and diversity. To the thousands of weekly papers and journals; to the little offset presses and portable duplicators of nameless number scattered in every town and hamlet turning out posters, pamphlets, handbills, and broadsides; to magazines overground and underground speaking the ideas of the respectable and the disreputable and aimed at whatever audience—churchgoers, atheists, lesbians, militant blacks or Ku Klux Klan whites, Puritan and prurient, reactionary or rebellious. Each of these is a part of the press, and the whole of it is all of them.

This American press, each part choosing what it will, can publish what it will. It can seize upon secrets stolen from government archives and broadcast them to the world. It can strip the

---

[8] Ibid. (document 27, p. 186).

privacy of councils and grand juries. It can pillory those accused of crimes before they are tried. It can heap calumnies not only upon elected governors but upon all whom chance has made an object of public attention. It can publish the lascivious and the sadistic. It can advance any opinion on any subject, including the opinion that all our government is corrupt and that the whole of the social order proclaimed in 1776 should be swept away and another put in its place.

This is unique, for such full freedom to publish exists nowhere else in the world. In many countries nothing can be published save with the imprimatur of some politburo. In others, the press has many of those freedoms. But in what other country is the press free to do all of these things with impunity? Even in that England which is the wellspring of our liberties there remain, after two hundred years, official secrets acts, strict libel laws, rigid rules on the reporting of judicial proceedings, and other restraints which put some limits upon the freedom of the press. In newer countries the authorities have taken early heed against too much license. Only in America are the boundaries of freedom so broad.

If, even in America, we have not yet extended the same freedom to the new electronic media it is due in part to the fact that for technological reasons there does not exist the multiplicity of outlets and so the same diversity is lacking. But it is also because these media are so newly upon us that there is no history to guide either public policy or media practice. We are just beginning to grapple with the political issues and philosophical conflicts that have long embroiled the printed press.

We have had some glimpse of those press conflicts and seen how they were resolved in our early days, at least partially, by argument and experience. In the century after the Sedition Act new spokesmen here and abroad came forward to expand thoughtfully and eloquently on the nature of civil liberty, notably John Stuart Mill. They provided a philosophical underpinning for a broader concept of freedom of the press.

At the same time the practical situation of the press continued to play its role. The proliferation of printing presses, the geographical expanse of the country and the separation of regions one from another, made for a diversity of political views—or at least a diversity of orthodoxies—and imposed very practical difficulties on the government in controlling the press even when it tried. With the western expansion across the continent this factor was intensified. The newspaper editor on the moving frontier was in practice answerable to no one for what he printed, except upon occasion to an irate reader with a horsewhip. He became accustomed to independence and fiercely defended it until gradually this independence became ever more deeply imbedded in the tradition of the craft.

Not, of course, that the government did not try to curtail it from time to time. In the Civil War President Lincoln, in defiance of the First Amendment, arrested the proprietors of *The New York World* and *The Journal of Commerce* for what seemed to him seditious libel. In peacetime President Theodore Roosevelt tried and failed to convict the *World* and *The Indianapolis News* for "a string of infamous libels," even sending a special message to Congress on the subject. These and other instances, some open, some more subtle, intensified the feeling among writers and printers that only eternal vigilance would preserve their laboriously won independence. Quite understandably, they continued to see government as an antagonist.

And not government alone. By the arrival of the twentieth century the complexities of an industrial society had created other centers of power seeming to the people as distant and even more mysterious and uncontrollable than government. In the shorthand of the day these were the "trusts," or Big Business, but in a larger sense they were all the institutions of society which have power but without clear-cut accountability. Thus there was ushered in the era of muckraking, at first aimed only at those "trusts" but gradually against other parts of the nongovernmental Establishment. The daily press—notably the papers of Hearst, Scripps and Pulitzer —took up the cudgels but the heaviest blows were struck by magazines such as *McClure's* and *Collier's,* and in books, both fiction and nonfiction. So the press began to acquire not merely an anti-government but an anti-institutional cast which remains with us yet.

Meanwhile, one by one the legal barriers against any restraints on the press toppled. The Fourteenth Amendment, as interpreted by the Supreme Court, extended the prohibition against press abridgment under the First Amendment to the states as well as to the national government. With the court's decision in *New York*

Times v. *Sullivan* private libel was, for all practical purposes, stricken from the law books; the press is not liable even for publishing falsehoods unless it can be proved that the intent was "malicious." In the Pentagon Papers case (*New York Times* v. *United States*) the press was allowed to publish stolen government documents without either restraint or liability.

We must not think, however, that efforts to put some limits on the freedom of the press were not often supported by public sentiment; to many people the press seems often to abuse its freedom to the injury of both individuals and society as a whole. Nor should we think that philosophy and reason are all on the side of untrammeled freedom. Thoughtful men have found moral, ethical and practical arguments for not letting liberty turn into license.

Let us go back for a moment and imagine how the argument for putting some restraints on the press might have been put by an articulate philosopher in the Crown colonies. It might have run something like this:

> Freedom of the press is essential to political liberty. Where men cannot freely convey their thoughts to one another no freedom is secure. But freedom of the press to appeal to reason may always be construed as freedom of the press to appeal to public passion and ignorance, vulgarity and cynicism. So it is always dangerous. The moral right of free public expression is not unconditional. When a man who claims the right is a liar, a prostitute whose political judgments can be bought, a dishonest inflamer of hatred and suspicion, his claim is groundless. To protect the press is not always to protect the community. Libel, obscenity, incitement to riot, sedition, these have a common principle; their utterance invades vital social interests. So the extension of legal sanctions to these categories of abuse is justified.

In fact, the above quotation is not imaginary. Every phrase of it is taken verbatim from the report of the Commission on Freedom of the Press, done in the twentieth century by a group of scholars and teachers, one of whom was an eminent philosopher and another the chancellor of the University of Chicago. No foes of liberty, they; no blind reactionaries, no partisan politicians. All of them thoughtful men, deeply disturbed by the fear that the abuse of liberty can destroy liberty.[9]

The report of the Commission on Freedom of the Press, more popularly known as the Hutchins commission, was issued in 1947. It was greeted by outraged outcries from the press, to whom it was heresy. And its import, without any question, was to challenge the absolutism of the idea of freedom of the press, threatening to take us back beyond Mill, beyond George Hay, beyond Madison and Jefferson and John Peter Zenger.

True, the Hutchins commission did not really grasp the nettle. That is, it did not say what ought to be done to restrain abuses of freedom of the press, or even who should be the judge of what they are, beyond the general thought that not every restraint on the press is wrong and some strong urgings that the press itself exercise self-restraint. But the commission did remind us that the nettle is there.

It always has been. The fundamental assumption of all who cherish freedom of the press and who have nourished it over the centuries is that it is the cornerstone of liberty. The safeguard of the citizens against tyranny is their freedom to remonstrate against despotic governors. A society of self-governing people is viable only if the people are informed. Men have no way of discovering the best ideas about man and God or man and society unless all ideas are free to confront each other, the good and the bad, in the cauldron of the intellectual marketplace. Without the right of free inquiry all other freedoms vanish. Such are the premises of free speech, from Milton to our own day.

Yet another assumption is that no man is free if he can be terrorized by his neighbor, whether by swords or by words; this is the justification of laws against violence and against libel and slander. Nor can a citizen be truly informed if falsehoods come masquerading as truth; false advertising for ideas is as injurious as those for foods or for drugs. Moreover the liberty of the citizen also depends upon the stability of society, which is why govern-

---

[9] Commission on Freedom of the Press, *A Free and Responsible Press* (Chicago: University of Chicago Press, 1947). Among the commission members were William E. Hocking, professor of philosophy at Harvard, and Robert M. Hutchins, then chancellor of the University of Chicago.

ments exist, and society has a right to protect itself against the predatory. Such are the premises of those who say no right is absolute, including freedom of the press, when it clashes with other rights.

Therein lies the nettle and it grows ever more prickly. If the right of a fair trial is fundamental to liberty, what happens to it if the press is free to prejudice a fair trial by what it publishes? If it is wrong for other institutions of society to have power without responsibility, is it right for the press—surely one of the more powerful institutions of society—to have no accountability for what it does?

These questions, raised a quarter of a century ago by the Hutchins commission, are now disturbing others. In that Pentagon Papers case the court reaffirmed the Blackstonian doctrine and refused to uphold prior restraint, but several of the judges were uneasy even with that as an absolute doctrine when it seemed to give sanction to the stealing of government documents. Justice White, for one, plainly said that while he would not restrain prior publication he might well sustain a decision holding the newspapers accountable for their actions as receivers of stolen property.

Within the press as well there is also a groping for some way to reconcile this freedom of the press with the other needs of liberty. A quarter century after the Hutchins commission there is much talk of press councils and other means of achieving both a free and responsible press. And two centuries after 1776 the reconciliation seems as difficult as ever.

Perhaps more so. For certainly the Founding Fathers would be astounded by how much we have enlarged the parameters of the debate. After all, when they met to draft the Constitution they did so in secret, barring the press entirely and pledging themselves to confidentiality of their discussions. They did so not because they feared open debate on their handiwork but because they saw values to liberty in the privacy of council. Certainly the purloining of state papers would have stirred even President Jefferson to outrage. None of them thought freedom of the press was a license to do anything whatever.

Yet the changes that time has wrought on the idea of freedom of the press were, I think, inevitable. Freedom of the press, once proclaimed, admits of no logical limit. If the national legislature may not abridge it, by what logic should state legislatures? If all ideas should be freely expressed, how can information on which ideas are based be suppressed? If government must be open, how can the governors keep secrets from the governed? And if the governors will not give information freely, is there not a right to wrest it from them? Each progression leads inexorably to the next.

In this country there has also been the pressure of historical experience, thrusting the boundaries ever outward. The very nature of our Revolution created a bias, first against distant government and then by extension against all government save that which governs least. Although the twentieth century has forced an acceptance of enlarged government, it has been a reluctant acceptance and it still divides the people. We remain unruly under the long arm of government, as when mothers parade to protest school busing or truck drivers block highways to protest fuel allocations. We remain equally suspicious of, and hostile to, other institutional sources of power.

This bias has been shared by those who report and comment on the news, and their habit of displaying it has been reinforced by the privilege of independence so fiercely fought for. "Print the news and raise hell"—that has been the traditional battle cry of the press. Except in rare moments it matters not who holds the power, what President the reins of governments, the press will soon be sniffing at his spoor and thundering at his actions.

That such freedom can be abused is undeniable. Good men can be slandered, justice thwarted, base passions aroused, people misinformed, government subverted, all the institutions of society undermined. It should surprise no one that there arise from time to time voices asking how we shall protect ourselves. As our society grows more complex these voices will, I am sure, grow more clamorous.

But this is true of all liberty. There is none that cannot be abused. And if the people cannot be trusted to find their way amid the abuses then there is no hope for the American experiment. For that experiment rests less upon logic than upon a faith that the danger of unbounded liberty is not so great as that of putting liberty in bondage. It is a faith so far justified. In our two hundred years we have been better served by our freedoms, including most especially our freedom of speech and of the press, than we would

20

have been served without them. That is the answer, perhap, only answer, to those who would no longer trust those freedom

All the same, the story is not ended. Freedom of religion. Freedom of person under the protection of habeas corpus. Trial by jury. Freedom of the press. "These principles," said Jefferson in his first Inaugural, "form the bright constellation which has gone before us, and guided our steps through an age of revolution and reformation." (Citation)

Freedom of religion, habeas corpus, trial by jury. All these have become so much a part of us we hardly remember that they were once things men fought over. Of that constellation only freedom of the press remains in the heat of controversy—as revolutionary an idea now as it was in the beginning.

Cover and book design: Pat Taylor